T0266365

LITTLE BOOK OF

YVES SAINT LAURENT

For Dusty Rose who really doesn't like knees.

I am indebted to my brilliant editor Issy Wilkinson for her wise observations, and many thanks to the excellent team at Welbeck.

Published in 2021 by Welbeck
An Imprint of HEADLINE PUBLISHING GROUP

12

Design and layout © 2021 Carlton Books Limited
Text © 2021 Emma Baxter-Wright

Cataloguing in Publication Data is available from the British Library
ISBN – 978-1-78739-554-1
Printed in China

HEADLINE PUBLISHING GROUP
An Hachette UK Company, Carmelite House
50 Victoria Embankment, London EC4Y 0DZ

www.headline.co.uk
www.hachette.co.uk

LITTLE BOOK OF

YVES SAINT LAURENT

The story of the iconic fashion designer

EMMA BAXTER-WRIGHT

WELBECK

CONTENTS

INTRODUCTION

"I felt myself drawn to the past, whilst the future drove me ahead."

YVES SAINT LAURENT

If the act of artistic genius requires equal amounts of talent and suffering, then Yves Saint Laurent, with an abundance of both firmly embedded in his DNA, successfully utilized these traits to propel his career from prodigious boy wonder to that of arguably the most influential designer of the twentieth century. With a career initially shaped by the traditions of haute couture, the designer had no hesitation in shaking off the shadow of his former employer Christian Dior and striking out in new directions to accommodate an era of change.

Recognized throughout his lifetime for a fragile disposition shielded behind trademark glasses, in truth his reclusive personality masked a steely determination to conquer the competition and secure iconic status as the author of modern womenswear. Saint Laurent made headlines in a life that was to become as mythologized as his dazzling designs: he scandalized

OPPOSITE The legendary couturier, known always as a great trailblazer, at the height of his success in 1976.

the world by posing naked to promote his own merchandise, shocked the fashion elite with trouser suits for women and transparent fabrics and solidified his international appeal by launching a range of ready-to-wear collections that democratized fashion for an audience of younger women. Innovation came from exploring new horizons in art and culture, from the perfect geometry of the Mondrian dress to the extravagant fantasy of the Opéras-Ballets Russes collection. Revered as a "legend", "God" and "idol" by every successful designer that trailed in his footsteps, and named by Coco Chanel as the rightful successor to her indisputable crown, Saint Laurent famously declared that his only regret in a visionary career was not to have invented blue jeans.

More than any other designer, Saint Laurent transcended the mere aesthetics of fashion and caused a revolution, trusting his instincts to empower women from the salon to the street through a seductive style that shaped the attitudes of the times.

ABOVE: As a young designer, scrutinizing the shape and silhouette of a toile in search of perfection.

OPPOSITE: An early example of a trouser suit designed for women, 1967.

EARLY LIFE

BUDDING TALENT

Surrounded by love, laughter and the shimmering heat of the
North African sun, Yves Henri Donat Mathieu-Saint-Laurent
was born into wealth and privilege in the melting-pot
cosmopolitan port of Oran, Algeria, on 1 August 1936.

*A*s the eldest of three children, with two younger
sisters, Michèle and Brigitte, the slight, shy boy with
a flashing smile was raised as a pampered prince of
the family, by Lucienne, his glamorous party-loving mother,
in an extended female household which included his maternal
grandmother, Madame Marianne Wilbaux, and Great-Aunt Renée.

His handsome, athletic father, Charles Mathieu-Saint-Laurent,
cut a distinguished figure in the town, overseeing an insurance
company and managing a string of cinemas in Algeria, Morocco
and Tunisia. Business often took him away from home, but
the relationship between father and son in a loving family
atmosphere was always strong, with the designer later recalling
him as "an exceptional human being". In summer, the family
decamped from their large three-storey house in Oran to their
villa in Trouville, one of the most prestigious coastal resorts in

OPPOSITE: Yves Saint Laurent at the age of 21, buttoned
up in a suit and tie, sporting the trademark glasses he
was rarely seen without.

the region, where for several months they swam in the ocean, picnicked on the beach and entertained friends for the season.

It was Lucienne, Yves' stylish mother, who encouraged her son's early artistic efforts and captivated the fertile imagination of the budding designer. He watched her dress up to dazzle café society, with her infectious laughter and innate good taste, and by the age of 13 he would accompany her each week to purchase the latest fashion magazines like *Vogue* and *Le Jardin des Modes* at the Manes bookstore. As he recounted when interviewed in the *Globe* in 1986, "When you live in the provinces, magazines from the capital are hugely important. At the time there were fantastic magazines about the theatre, and also fashion magazines with designs by people like Bérard, Dalí, Cocteau. Those magazines had an enormous influence on me."

This visually tantalizing peek into the possibilities of an

RIGHT: With his glamorous mother Lucienne Mathieu-Saint-Laurent, the first woman Yves designed dresses for.

altogether different type of existence was reinforced in May 1950 when the teenager was taken to the municipal opera house in Oran to see a performance of Molière's *L'École des femmes* (School for Wives) with sets and costumes designed by Christian Bérard. Enthralled by the spectacle of this early theatrical exposure, Saint Laurent later claimed: "It was an extraordinarily emotional experience, the most extraordinary I have ever had." The magical illusion of the theatre consumed an impressionable young Yves and thinking this could be where his professional future lay, he invented a fantasy world in which he immersed himself. His parents provided a room for him, where, as self-appointed director, set designer and couturier, he staged secret performances by invitation only for his sisters. As creative mastermind for his productions, Yves painted scenic backdrops and invented cut-out cardboard characters dressed in fabric costumes made with scraps cut from his mother's gowns.

In sharp contrast to this idyllic home life where he was cherished as the blue-eyed boy, the Jesuit-Catholic boarding school he attended from the age of 12 provided him with nothing but ongoing misery. As a pale and timid outsider, who spent his free time alone without friends, Yves' teenage years were marked with trauma and unhappiness as he juggled a dual existence: " On the one hand there was the cheerful life with my family, the world I created with my drawings, costumes and plays. On the other, the ordeal of Catholic school, where I was an outcast." Years later, he told *Le Figaro* that he suffered the horrific beating and bullying at school knowing he was different to the other boys and that one day he would be famous. A passion for reading Marcel Proust, and a developing interest in the seasonal collections of the Parisian designers Hubert de Givenchy, Christian Dior and Cristóbal Balenciaga, all served as

At home in Oran, an adolescent Yves spent hours immersed in a fantasy world of fashion, creating hundreds of outfits for his paper dolls based on models of the 1950s.

ABOVE: Saint Laurent in Paris, with his winning design for the International Wool Secretariat competition in 1954. Karl Lagerfeld, who was awarded second prize, is on the left.

welcome distractions from the terror of the playground.

From 1951 onward, Yves spent hours filling sketchbooks with sets and costumes for the ballet and theatre, transcribing books, illustrating text and providing detailed drawings for the ensembles worn by fictional characters such as Madame Bovary and Scarlett O'Hara. As well as designing outfits for his mother, which were given to her seamstress to make up, Yves created his own fashion collections using paper dolls he had made in the guise of Suzy Parker and Bettina Graziani, the most famous mannequins of the day. The imaginative wardrobes he invented for 11 paper dolls were extensive, producing over 500 different garments and accessories, and writing detailed programme notes to accompany each collection. The young artist always signed and dated his work "YMSL" or "Yves Mathieu-Saint Laurent" and only later, around 1957, dropped the Mathieu and settled on the signature "YSL".

Encouraged by his family, Yves submitted work into the International Wool Secretariat fashion competition, and in autumn 1953 set off for Paris with his mother, Lucienne, to collect third prize. Through his father's contacts he was introduced to the influential magazine editor Michel de Brunhoff during his short stay in the capital. De Brunhoff, who had founded *Gazette du bon ton*, and now edited *Vogue (Paris)*, was very impressed with what he saw. Recognizing Yves' flair for fashion, he encouraged him to keep drawing but also to finish his baccalaureate exams. When college was over, de Brunhoff suggested Yves enrol at the Ecole de la Chambre Syndicale de la Couture Parisienne, the best fashion school in Paris, to improve his couture technique. His parents agreed and at 18, he began a new life in the capital, renting a furnished room at 209 Boulevard Pereire in the 17th arrondissement. Later that year, competing with 6,000 other entrants, Yves won first prize for his elegant designs in the dress category of the 1954 International Wool Secretariat competition, where his winning design – a black wool cocktail dress which provided an early example of his instinctive eye for wearable style – was made up in the atelier of Hubert de Givenchy.

His victory was reported in the local paper, *L'Echo d'Oran*, but despite this early validation of success, Yves was suffering from what would be the first of many bouts of depression. Recognizing the unhappiness in his son, Charles Mathieu-Saint-Laurent wrote in confidence to Michel de Brunhoff to ask again for his help. After a productive holiday in Oran, Yves returned to the offices of *Vogue* in Paris armed with 50 original sketches to show de Brunhoff his latest work. Stunned by the similarity of his drawings to those of Christian Dior's new A-line collection he had seen the previous day, the journalist telephoned his great friend and arranged a time to introduce his talented protégé to the feted designer. The meeting was a great success and on 20 June 1955, the boy from Oran who fantasized about working for Christian Dior, the greatest couturier in Paris, realized his dream.

SUCCESSOR TO CHRISTIAN DIOR

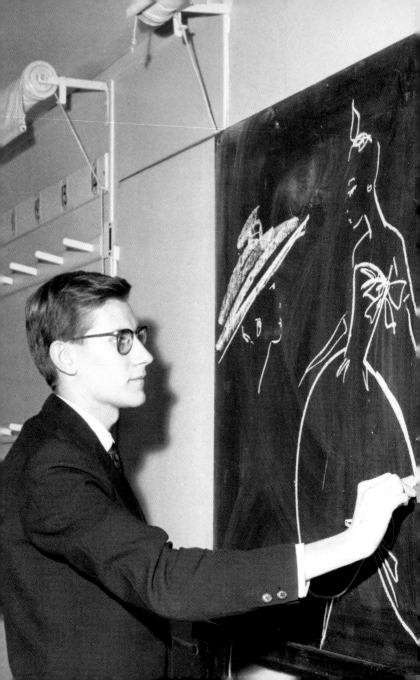

HEIR TO
THE THRONE

Stepping through the hallowed doors of 30 Avenue Montaigne
for his first day at work as an apprentice, Saint Laurent began
the important process of learning how to run a successful
couture house from the bottom up.

T he Parisian fashion house had a global reputation, thanks
to the unrivalled success of Christian Dior's post-war
silhouette of glamorous femininity, which he called
La Ligne Corolle and which Carmel Snow, editor of American
Harper's Bazaar, dubbed the "New Look". In a single collection
Dior's international fame had been assured and when a painfully
shy Saint Laurent arrived at the Maison eight years later, Dior
was widely acknowledged as the most celebrated and financially
successful couturier in the world.

Owned by Marcel Boussac, then the wealthiest man in France,
the company employed around 1,000 people, owned 27 ateliers
and was responsible for nearly half of all haute couture exports
to America. Royalty, Hollywood's A-List and the best-dressed

OPPOSITE: An extraordinarily gifted illustrator, seen here sketching
early designs on a chalkboard at the House of Dior in the early 60s.

ABOVE: One of the last photos taken of Yves Saint Laurent with his mentor Christian Dior, backstage at a fashion show in 1957.

women in the world all clamoured to be adorned by Monsieur Dior. His enviable client list included Elizabeth Taylor, Margot Fonteyn, Marlene Dietrich and Wallis, Duchess of Windsor, as well as the aristocratic beauties Gloria Guinness and Daisy Fellowes.

Dressed in a white lab coat and working each day from a wooden desk in the studio, Yves was soon promoted to the role of assistant with Marc Bohan and Guy Douvier, then elevated to principal associate, working directly alongside Christian Dior. The *Maison* operated under a strict hierarchy, with a rigorous structure that ensured everyone knew their place and what was expected of them within the townhouse premises. To rise up through the ranks to reach the level of premiére was a great honour and demanded the dedication of around 20 years of work that was continually examined and graded for elegance, finishing and execution. As head of a successful couture house, Dior was under pressure. Although celebrated as the most famous couturier in the world, the ongoing expectations to excite an international audience of clients and press at every new show had become a relentless treadmill and the designer was quick to recognize and value the assured competence of his youthful employee. Yves' first sketches dated from July 1955 remain in the Dior archives and his mentor began to include his designs in the bi-annual shows from as early as autumn of that year. For his part, Yves admired his new boss immensely, was thrilled to learn his professional craft within the confines of such a prestigious environment and felt the individual creativity of both men benefited from working closely with one another.

"I arrived in the morning and spent the day alongside Christian Dior without talking very much. I have to say that I learned a great deal. Christian Dior overstimulated the imagination, and he trusted me totally with his work. One of his ideas would give me ideas, and one of my ideas might give him ideas. There was no discussion between us. I had an idea. I drew it. I showed him the sketch. The big demonstration between us was the proof. Since I am not talkative, I prefer that, it's a *tour de force*."

Influential tastemaker Carmel Snow picked up on one of Yves' early designs for Dior and included it in her 1955 "Paris Report" for the September issue of American *Harper's Bazaar*. *Soirée de Paris*, an elegant black sheath dress with contrast satin bow, was modelled by the aristocratic beauty Dovima and captured on film by the genius young photographer Richard Avedon in a sensational photographic setting at the Cirque d'Hiver in Paris. The classic fashion photograph that went on to become an iconic image of understated 1950s style set a record price for an Avedon photo when it sold at Christie's Auction House for $1.2 million in November 2010.

Yves was happy in his new role in an atmosphere that was reassuringly familiar to him, surrounded by a predominantly female workforce, the majority of whom were much older than him. Neatly buttoned up in a uniform of charcoal grey suits, sporting cropped school-boy hair and wire framed specs, the conservative youth had found a few allies of his own age and started to socialize with them after work. Anne-Marie Muñoz, a family friend of Dior's who had started off as a messenger in the workrooms and worked her way up, and the unconventional model Victoire Doutreleau, whose Saint Germain looks made her Dior's favourite muse, were both strong women who would remain friends and later participate in the opening of Saint Laurent's own haute couture house.

Having gained Dior's trust, Yves found an increasing number of his original designs included in every collection, with the grand couturier openly praising the skills of his young associate. In July 1957, the designer celebrated 10 years of success for the fashion house that bore his name. He made the cover of *Time* magazine brandishing a giant pair of cutting shears and told his business partner, Jacques Rouet, "Yves Saint Laurent is young, but he is an immense talent. In my last collection, I consider him to be the father of 34 out of the 180 designs. I think the time has come to reveal it to the press. My prestige won't suffer from it."

When Lucienne came to visit her son in Paris that year she was summoned by Monsieur Dior, who had asked to meet her. She spoke later of the encounter: "He made some complimentary remarks and then said, 'Yves is the one who'll succeed me.' At the time I didn't really understand. Dior was still young, 60 at most."

If the great Dior had vocalized his desire that Yves had been chosen to eventually succeed him, it was understood as something to be considered in the future when his protégé had matured into the role, not as a premonition forecasting his imminent demise. The wider world, however, was unaware that despite outward appearances of a calm demeanour, the couturier was riddled with

OPPOSITE: A triumphant debut collection for Christian Dior in 1957, featuring a new, less structured silhouette called the "trapeze" line.

anxiety and consumed by health worries about his weight. While taking an autumn trip to his spa clinic in Montecatini Terme, Italy, Dior collapsed suddenly and died of a heart attack, aged 52. The fashion world mourned the death of a man seen as the heroic saviour of Parisian couture and his funeral was attended by vast crowds and famous couturiers Pierre Balmain, Cristóbal Balenciaga and Hubert de Givenchy.

The unexpected death of Dior catapulted the frail-looking 21-year-old Yves centre stage into the reluctant role of successor. There was much deliberation as to whether the young pretender was mature enough to withstand the pressures demanded by the House of Dior, but Marcel Boussac, the industrialist billionaire who financed the company, was hesitant to close the door on a business that turned over two billion francs. On 15 November, 1957, a press conference was called at Avenue Montaigne, where business partner Jacques Rouet made the announcement to the assembled audience that the couture house would be run by a creative team consisting of four individuals, all of whom had been hired personally by Monsieur Dior: Madame Zehnacker, Marguerite Carré, Mitzah Bricard and Yves Saint Laurent. The news was well received by the French press, with the evening paper *Paris-Presse-L'intransigeant* printing congratulatory headlines: "The Invisible Yves Saint Laurent Was Tonight Crowned Christian Dior's Successor".

As was his usual custom, after the announcement Yves rushed back home to his family in Oran, where he locked himself away in his room and completed over 600 original sketches in 15 days for the upcoming collection. When he returned to Paris, the longstanding team of Zehnacker, Carré and Bricard edited a legion of fresh ideas into a streamlined collection of 178 looks dominated by a fluid silhouette that swung jauntily from shoulder to knee.

On the day of the show, 30 January 1958, Yves waited nervously backstage with a sprig of lily of the valley (Christian Dior's favourite good luck charm) in his buttonhole. His debut collection – called the "Trapeze" – relied on none of Dior's signature stiffening and padding. Instead, Yves' youthful line liberated female curves from the tyranny of a nipped-in waistline and skimmed the body in a similar style to that of Balenciaga's iconic "baby doll" dress. The applause was immediate, the collection hailed a triumph and Yves woke to find glowing headlines around the world, claiming Saint Laurent "has saved France".

Within weeks of his successful debut, Yves met the man who was to become a lifelong soulmate, partner, protector and tireless promoter in the years that lay ahead. At 27, Pierre Bergé was the opposite of Saint Laurent in almost every respect – short, ebullient, energetic and ruthlessly controlling, a man determined

RIGHT: Yves Saint Laurent inspects his Beat collection for Christian Dior 1960, in the salon at 30 Avenue Montaigne.

OPPOSITE: The collection that made Yves Saint Laurent the "saviour of France" in 1957, exemplified by strong colour and an overall sense of fluidity.

to succeed in life whatever the costs. The couple were introduced at a dinner party given by the influential fashion editor and high society hostess Marie-Louise Bousquet. At the time Bergé was the lover and enthusiastic business supporter of the artist Bernard Buffet, but as his star faded and an acrimonious break up followed, Bergé had already discovered a new artist to champion. The pair made an unlikely double act and yet the combination of their respective talents created a dynamic and enduring partnership that went on to conquer the world of fashion for the next five decades.

Yves trusted his instincts for the next few collections he produced for Dior, with designs that reflected a more youthful spirit than that of his predecessor. Influenced enormously by Coco Chanel, who believed women wanted freedom of movement without constraints, he declared in the press release for his spring/ summer 1959 Longue collection, "Line has been sacrificed to the benefit of style." For his Beat collection of 1960, he took inspiration from the French actress and cabaret singer Juliette Gréco and the beatniks who hung around the jazz clubs of Saint-Germain-des-Prés, producing an entirely black collection of ultra-modern clothes that included motorcycle jackets in alligator, mink coats with knitted sleeves, turtleneck cashmere sweaters and tight knit caps. This bold style statement was greeted with astonishment from a slightly bewildered Dior clientele and did little to impress Marcel Boussac, who was so alarmed at the customers' reaction that when Saint Laurent was conscripted into the army later that year, the House of Dior did not contest it.

The timid 24-year-old was drafted to fight in the Algerian colonial war but collapsed during the induction process and was sent briefly to a military hospital before being transferred for further treatment to Val de Grâce, a mental hospital in southern Paris. After a relentless campaign by Pierre Bergé to get him out, he was finally released from hospital in November 1960 and discharged from the army due to ill health. The impact of this terrifying ordeal, where he was given electric shock treatment and heavily sedated with a cocktail of psychoactive drugs, would scar for life a fragile man already prone to episodes of neuroses.

During this time Yves discovered he no longer had a job waiting for him at the House of Dior, who did not renew his contract and had instead appointed Marc Bohan to take over. Physically and mentally diminished by his recent hospital experiences but determined to start a new venture, Yves relied increasingly on the support of his partner to deal with the court case against Dior for breach of contract and to raise funds to finance his own couture house. Pierre Bergé took control of everything. He helped Yves settle back into his apartment on rue Vauban, successfully sued Dior for damages and raised additional finance from J. Mack Robinson, an entrepreneur from Atlanta, Georgia.

With just enough funding to make a start, the House of Yves Saint Laurent was officially launched on 4 December 1961, with the first couture show presented in January the following year from their newly acquired premises at 30 bis rue Spontini.

OPPOSITE: The Beat collection included a significant amount of soft leather, patent crocodile skin and dark colours. This was the final collection Yves Saint Laurent produced for the House, as it was considered too edgy for the sedate clientele of Dior.

ARTISTIC
EXPLOSION OF
COLOUR

WEARABLE
WORKS OF ART

"Contrary to what people might think, the severe lines of
Mondrian's pictures worked well on the female form. The
results provoked a sensation."

YVES SAINT LAURENT, PARIS MATCH, 1981

T he eminent graphic designer Cassandre created a logo
for the new company, a stylish monogram that consisted
of the initials of Yves Saint Laurent's name sensuously
intertwined in a style that reflected the modernist approach of
his haute couture house. Many Dior employees switched their
allegiance and started working for Saint Laurent, including the
very capable Anne-Marie Muñoz, who became a key figure and
went on to manage the studio for the next 40 years.

The public immediately saw a change of mood from the young
man who, working under his own name, had no obligations
to adhere to the traditional demands of the past. New shapes
and silhouettes tumbled out of him and onto his catwalk. The
double-breasted pea coat (*le caban*), wide-legged "sailor" trousers,

OPPOSITE: Saint Laurent's homage to the Dutch painter
Piet Mondrian provided huge international success for the designer
in his 1965 Autumn/Winter collection.

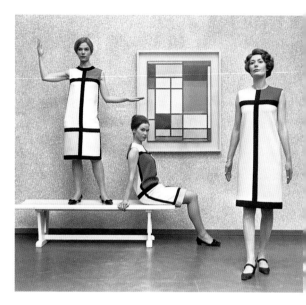

RIGHT: Superb cutting techniques were utilized to keep the geometry of the grid lines intact, with a variety of Mondrian-themed dresses produced, using different blocks of colour, and design.

simple tunic shifts, short evening dresses and a stylish trench coat all made their debut within a couple of seasons.

The company was a success as a youthful Saint Laurent could be relied upon to deliver a stylish injection of "street" in terms of practical modernism, while still maintaining the established principles of superb execution and finishing learnt through his training in Dior's couture salon. Saint Laurent (like some of his contemporaries) was quick to recognize the cultural shifts in society and women's changing role within it. He picked up on the phenomenal success of Mary Quant in London, acknowledged the futuristic space age outfits presented by Courrèges in 1964 and consequently understood the importance of creating something that would appeal to a younger generation who were rebelling against the long-established conventions of formal fashion. Several weeks before finalizing the line-up for his 1965 Autumn/

Winter show, Saint Laurent surveyed his work, decided it lacked modernism and set about re-designing brand new outfits: "I was getting bogged down in traditional elegance and Courrèges yanked me out of it. His collection stimulated me. I said to myself, I can come up with something better."

The catalyst that sparked the process of producing "something better" came from a book his mother, Lucienne, had recently given him. While leafing through Michel Seuphor's 1957 book, *Piet Mondrian: Life and Work*, a definitive biography about the abstract art and neoplastic style of the Dutch artist Piet Mondrian (1872–1944), Saint Laurent was struck by the idea that fashion needed to provide women with a new type of functional elegance more suited to contemporary life.

"I suddenly realized that dresses should no longer be composed of lines, but colours. I realized that we had to stop conceiving of a garment as sculpture and that, on the contrary, we had to view it as a mobile. I realized that fashion had been rigid up till then, and that we now have to make it move."

Taking inspiration from the geometric lines and asymmetric use of block colour exemplified by Mondrian and from the jigsaw paintings of the Russian-born French modernist Serge Poliakoff (1900–69), Saint Laurent produced 26 new designs which clearly paid homage to both men's artistic work and seamlessly transposed the visual dynamic of a two-dimensional painting into modern fashion. Constructed in fluid wool jersey from the House of Racine, the Mondrian-inspired collection consisted of perfectly proportioned straight shift dresses which incorporated primary colours, separated by black grid lines on a predominantly white background. Saint Laurent's genius lay in his skill in keeping the lines and colour blocks of Mondrian's paintings apparently geometrically aligned on the moveable shape of a woman's body, which he achieved by imperceptibly incorporating darts and seams

LEFT: Trompe-l'oeil pop art dresses inspired directly from Tom Wesselmann's Great American Nude series were interpreted into swinging sixties fashion for the Autumn/Winter collection in 1966.

into the graphic grid shapes. The fact that the ideal model figure in the 1960s was stick-thin without the obstacle of either rounded hips or a curvaceous bosom to distort the bold geometry of his designs certainly worked in his favour in the flawless execution of pared-down elegance.

The outfits were an immediate success story with both press and clientele, and marked a significant moment in the history of fashion. The "Ligne Mondrian" was hailed as groundbreaking and the global applause that followed did much to boost the reputation of both designer and artist, with copies of the dress produced all over the world. As a direct result of the publicity, a retrospective of Mondrian's work was held at the Musée de l'Orangerie in Paris a few years later. Sales to buyers took off and revenue for the house increased from 790,000 to 1.4 million francs in one season. Interviewed by a Sunday newspaper on the decision to take such a radical change of direction, Saint Laurent explained he was simply "fed up with making dresses for blasé billionaires."

The Mondrian dress kick-started an artistic theme that Saint Laurent would go on to explore in many inventive forms over the coming years. As a designer who was passionate about culture, who loved opera, ballet and the theatre, his antennae were finely tuned to the changing moods of abstraction and the American Op Art and Pop Art movements of the mid-sixties provided him with expressive new ways to translate a canvas to the catwalk. His collections for 1966 drew heavily on new pieces by Andy Warhol, Roy Lichtenstein, Tom Wesselmann and Bridget Riley. Working with an exceptionally vibrant colour palette and the visual witticisms of cut-out trompe-l'oeil profiles, as well as monochrome Op Art techniques, Saint Laurent produced Pop Art cocktail dresses with bubble-gum pink hearts, sun and moon motifs and graphic black and white chevrons styled into short,

OPPOSITE: Birds in flight were a favourite motif of the artist Georges Braque, re-interpreted into haute couture fashion by Yves Saint Laurent for his Spring/Summer 1988 collection.

RIGHT: Contemporary art remained an enduring influence throughout Saint Laurent's life, with the couturier adopting the symbolism of cubism from Georges Braque's guitar along with doves into a spectacular evening dress.

ABOVE: Detail of the exquisite embroidery and bead detailing produced by the House of Lesage for Yves Saint Laurent, to recreate the vibrance of Van Gogh's irises and sunflowers.

OPPOSITE PAGE: Naomi Campbell and Bess Stonehouse walk the runway in lavish Vincent van Gogh-inspired evening jackets, embellished with thousands of sequins and tiny seed pearls, for Spring/ Summer 1988.

sharp daywear. Most memorable were two outfits inspired by Wesselmann's *Great American Nude series*, which perfectly transposed the language of the Pop Art movement into sublime fashion. The visually fluid evening gown with its pink trompe-l'oeil profile of a woman's body that falls asymmetrically from shoulder to floor inlaid seamlessly in purple wool jersey is a masterclass in understated style.

Over the course of a 40-year career, Saint Laurent consistently revisited the idea that fashion and art were irrevocably linked, taking inspiration from the glittering colours of the Opéras-Ballets Russes collection in 1976, Picasso's cubism interpreted into flamboyant multicoloured satin appliqué dresses in 1979 and paid tribute to Louis Aragon and Jean Cocteau by embroidering lines of their poetry onto sumptuous bejewelled satin evening jackets in 1980. The Spring/Summer collection of 1988 was highly praised for its extraordinary beaded appliqué motifs produced in collaboration with the House of Lesage, headed up by François Lesage. The Van Gogh "Iris" cardigan made using 250,000 sequins and 200,000 individually threaded pearls in 22 different colours was just one example of Yves' masterful homage to the great twentieth-century artists.

A DECADE
OF STYLE
INNOVATION

THE STYLISH 1960s

"Fashions fade, style is eternal. My dream is to provide women
with the foundations of a classic wardrobe that escapes
the fashion of the moment, giving them greater confidence
in themselves."

YVES SAINT LAURENT

Saint Laurent had initiated a soaring trajectory that saw
his status rocket from ambitious young pretender to the
most influential designer in the world. He revolutionized
the way women thought about clothes, producing a series of
sensational innovations, many of which took inspiration from
classic menswear items and went on to become modern fashion
staples, such as the double-breasted reefer jacket or the trouser
suit. Like Coco Chanel, who had enhanced the reputation of her
own label by embracing her role as a celebrity figurehead, the
success of Saint Laurent's brand was magnified by a fascination
about the mythical stature of the man himself. Although buoyed
by his success and embracing a 1960s vibe of longer hair and
casual clothes, he continued to smoke incessantly and regularly
found himself derailed by debilitating dark depressions and
mental fragility.

OPPOSITE: With longer hair, and a bohemian style of dress, Yves Saint Laurent poses
for a CBS fashion special in June 1968, wearing sunglasses and a leather trench coat,
from his new collection of menswear.

Throughout his career, rumours of sickness and addiction propelled the public appetite for designer as introverted artist tortured by his own talent, a troubling image of genius which has never been so commercially utilized before or since.

Shielded by his partner Pierre Bergé from the day-to-day financial complexities of running the business, Saint Laurent was part of a fashionable set who regularly dined at Maxim's and later danced till the early hours at Régine's night club in the Latin Quarter. But his existence was not just one of gilded ivory tower entitlement, he was astute to the social changes in society and as *Vogue* journalist Hamish Bowles later observed, "Saint Laurent captured the zeitgeist with uncanny acuity".

Saint Laurent understood women. He hung out with his female friends, Betty Catroux (a tall, androgynous blonde who many claimed was the female double of the designer himself and was also his muse), Clara Saint, a Chilean heiress who went on to run the Rive Gauche press office, and Anne-Marie Muñoz. Through them he understood the need for clothing that empowered women in a society increasingly dominated by a female voice that demanded equality.

Though fully committed to the exacting processes involved in haute couture, Saint Laurent also recognized the limitations of a collection that was labour-intensive and prohibitively expensive to all but a few. The audience of women worldwide who could afford to spend thousands of pounds on a bespoke evening gown or hand-stitched, jewel-encrusted cocktail dress was dwindling before his eyes, while he felt himself part of a younger generation who took their cues from the spirit of the street. Inspired by the fast-moving world he could sense unfolding around him, Saint Laurent was on a mission to provide a viable and stylish alternative for those who could not afford his extremely expensive haute couture clothes. He was not the first couturier

OPPOSITE: Embracing his constant companions Betty Catroux and Loulou de la Falaise, in matching safari tunics, at the opening of the Rive Gauche boutique on Bond Street, London.

RIGHT: This understated cotton shirt dress with hooped chain belt typified the new younger style, worn with pilgrim buckle low-heeled pumps designed by Roger Vivier for Yves Saint Laurent.

OPPOSITE: French actress Catherine Deneuve modelling a double-breasted plaid wool trouser suit, from Yves Saint Laurent's prêt-à-porter collection on sale in the new Rive Gauche boutique in Paris. Her endorsement ensured it became an instant bestseller.

to offer ready-to-wear fashion – Madeleine Vionnet (1876–1975) and Lucien Lelong (1889–1958) both toyed with the idea of selling less expensive, off-the-peg ranges – but Saint Laurent was the first to develop the concept fully, defining the unique characteristics of each line with the explanation, "Rive Gauche is for the necessities, for the needs of daily life. In haute couture you can allow yourself to dream." His ambition to provide a collection of seasonal prêt-à-porter clothes in his signature designs made from quality fabrics with excellent production values was brought to life with the first Saint Laurent Rive Gauche boutique, which opened its doors at 21 rue de Tournon, on the Left Bank of Paris, on 26 September, 1966.

Situated in the narrow streets around Église Saint-Sulpice, off Boulevard Saint-Germain, the new boutique designed by Isabel Heybey was painted with red and black lacquered ceilings and featured tubular Mies van der Rohe chairs to create a modernist but functional aesthetic. The "Rive Gauche" clothes, which were manufactured by sewing machine rather than handstitched, referenced similar themes to those shown in his couture collections but were not simply a cheaper, watered-down version. The ready-to-wear range allowed the couture rebel to express a more carefree attitude, targeted specifically to a generation who could not afford to indulge in the elitism of bespoke fashion, while his creative process remained intact: "The big difference between couture and ready-to-wear is not design. It is the fabrics, the handwork and the fittings. The act of creation is the same," the designer explained to *Women's Wear Daily* in 1968.

The new boutique featured a life-size portrait of Saint Laurent surveying his new venture in trademark suit and statement glasses, painted by the artist Eduardo Arroyo (1937–2018). Striped jersey dresses hung from the shop walls, while dazzling jewellery trinkets and accessories were presented in gleaming metal-and-glass display cabinets. Guest of honour at the grand opening was 23-year-old blonde beauty Catherine Deneuve, a young French actress whom Saint Laurent first encountered a year earlier when she approached him to design a dress for her to wear at a reception hosted by the Queen of England. In movie-star style, she arrived wearing oversized sunglasses, her glossy hair drawn back with a velvet hairband, dressed in a military-style pea coat with statement buttons. Saint Laurent helped her pick out some suede miniskirts and a new trouser suit, which quickly became a bestseller.

The "Rive Gauche" line was an immediate hit as young women seized the chance to own a little piece of Parisian style

ABOVE: At the opening of his first prêt-à-porter Rive Gauche boutique in Rue de Tournon situated on the Left Bank in Paris, with models wearing matching skinny knit minidresses and hooped chain belts, September 1966.

created by the genius of Yves Saint Laurent with a price tag they could afford. The shop became a go-to location for a complete look of designer separates, accessories, jewellery and shoes that could all be tried on in situ and bought on the spot. The concept to roll out a chain of Rive Gauche boutiques to the fashion capitals around the world began in 1968 with a ready-to-wear boutique that opened on Madison Avenue, New York, followed in 1969 by one in Bond Street, London. That year, the designer also turned his attention to creating a similar vein of contemporary modern menswear with the launch of his first Saint Laurent Rive Gauche collection for men. The Parisian boutique situated alongside his womenswear shop in rue de

Tournon provided a relaxed style of clothing that broke away from the traditional conformity of tailored suits.

Rejecting stereotypical menswear in favour of a newfound freedom of expression, the shop stocked patterned silk shirts, knitted twinsets, velvet jackets and easy trench coats, all of which reflected Saint Laurent's own wardrobe choices. The new venture proved as successful as the womenswear line, snapped up by an army of uninhibited young men ready to explore their own identity through a more flamboyant style of dress appropriate for the era. Less than 20 years later, there were nearly 200 Saint Laurent Rive Gauche boutiques worldwide.

From the inception of his own House, Saint Laurent experienced a whirlwind burst of creativity, exploring a wide range of influences that helped consolidate his personal fame and professional reputation. Decades earlier, Chanel – whom he admired greatly – had successfully re-appropriated menswear for women and now Saint Laurent also looked outside traditional female tropes to create new genres of clothing appropriate for the era's burgeoning sexual revolution. He dressed women in an elegant trench coat, designed trousers for day- and evening wear, feminized a gentleman's traditional after-dinner jacket for an androgynous female figure and borrowed military-style uniforms to create his iconic "Saharienne" safari jacket.

Each collection presented a fresh challenge to the established norms of good taste and all of his innovations consistently reinforced the ethos that women should be allowed the same freedom of movement as men. These visionary pieces celebrated at the time and ultimately recognized as Saint Laurent "classics" were referenced and reinterpreted many times over throughout his long career with the designer acknowledging "good things never go out of fashion".

RIGHT: Yves Saint Laurent produced endless variations of his trouser suit, taking a classic male uniform and re-appropriating for women, tweaking proportions, fabrics and details to revolutionize the way women wanted to be seen in an era of sexual ambiguity.

LEFT: A 1967 example of Le Smoking, the black tuxedo jacket that went on to become a recognized House of Yves Saint Laurent staple for the next four decades.

OPPOSITE: Known as a rebel couturier who loved to surprise and shock his audience, here the classic Le Smoking is re-invented with wool Bermuda shorts, mixing masculine and feminine tropes with the addition of a totally transparent, pussy bow blouse.

LEFT: Diana Ross, lead singer of the Motown girl group The Supremes, radiates glamour in fluid velvet pants and a belted tunic top to celebrate the arrival of the Rive Gauche boutique in New York, 1968.

Designed to make women feel powerful, Saint Laurent provided a modern alternative to a traditional evening gown when he first presented his black tuxedo jacket known as "Le Smoking" in 1966. Superb cutting of a masculine trouser suit juxtaposed with overtly feminine pussy bow silk shirts played with topical ideas of sexual ambiguity and, initially, the elegant tuxedo caused outrage, with women who wore his trouser suits refused service in hotels and restaurants. Nobody looked better in Le Smoking than his best friend Betty Catroux, whose slim, androgynous frame and angular features exemplified the trend for unisex style, and the success of his tuxedo would transcend all other designs to become the most recognized signature of his whole career.

Le Smoking went through many evolutions, initially worn with a white blouse and black wool trousers stitched with a wide satin side stripe along the outside leg. Two years later, it appeared with tailored Bermuda shorts and a totally transparent black blouse, creating another round of shockwaves and publicity. A range of sheer organza shift dresses exquisitely decorated with sequinned ribbons embellishing strategic points at the breast and lower torso also caused controversy.

In 1968, when Paris was rocked by student protests, Saint Laurent escaped to Marrakesh for several months, returning to present a collection full of audacity that paid homage to the riots by featuring a series of duffel coats and fringed leather jackets, as well as his daring black chiffon "see-through dress" that bared everything but revealed very little by virtue of an extravagant band of ostrich feathers positioned strategically around the hips.

Born in North Africa, the designer found an ongoing source of inspiration in the art and culture of the continent. His Bambara collection consisted of beaded and bejewelled

RIGHT: Sales of the
trouser suit were
boosted by the
endorsement of
celebrity fans like
French actress
Brigitte Bardot,
seen here in a classic
double-breasted suit.

LEFT: The 1967 Spring/Summer collection dre~ inspiration from the ar~ of Africa, with a series ~ intricately beaded min~ dresses and elaborate headdresses.

OPPOSITE: In 1968, Yv~ Saint Laurent shocked audiences with the near total nudity of th~ transparent evening dress, trimmed only with a band of ostrich feathers around the hi~ and a Claude Lalanne gold serpent belt.

mini shifts, intricately appliquéd with jet and bronze coloured wooden beads, sequins and decorated with raffia. While a problematic style looked at through the lens of the present day, imbued as it is with its history of colonialism, Saint Laurent's "safari" or utility jacket – inspired by the gaberdine uniforms worn by military troops in Africa – was first debuted in the 1967 runway show to much acclaim. It was however a bespoke gaberdine utility tunic with metal ring belt made specifically for *Vogue Paris* the following year that caused an editorial sensation, shown on the statuesque six-foot German model Veruschka in a scrubland location shot by photographer Franco Rubartelli. The sexually powerful image captured the female liberation zeitgeist and ensured an avalanche of customers when the mass-produced version arrived on the Rive Gauche rails.

Trouser suits were a Saint Laurent staple in all forms, but as the decade progressed, the designer introduced an elegant jumpsuit into his repertoire, the basis of which came from the functionality of an all-in-one aviator suit. Embracing the practicality of the utilitarian workwear, he redesigned the concept as womenswear, replacing the original baggy silhouette with a refined cut that emphasized the shape of the female body. Immediately successful with the cigarette-slim models of the day, his new jumpsuit was produced in many versions, in fabrics ranging from sparkling sequins to demure wool jersey, and with a multitude of different design details. The new Saint Laurent creation was a particular hit with the American customers, who appreciated both the practicality and comfort of the jumpsuit. Within weeks, the New York boutique was out of stock.

From stylized versions of the practical pea coat to breaking the taboo of nudity, the design innovations debuted in this period anticipated the evolving roles of women within the context of a tumultuous period of change.

RIGHT: The first jumpsuits appeared on the runway in 1968, originally inspired by the functional all-in-one aviator suits worn by pilots. This version made in crepe de chine with flared pants and a revealing zip fastener could be worn for day or evening.

THE SCANDALOUS 70s

THE ERA OF LIBERATION

Internationally famous and seen as an integral part of the elite jet set crowd, Saint Laurent in his early thirties appeared to be more at ease with himself and his newfound image as celebrity couturier.

Paparazzi snaps capture him partying in New York with Andy Warhol, hanging out with Rudolf Nureyev at the hedonistic Club Sept in Paris and spending time with a revolving group of wealthy bohemians centred around John Paul Getty Jr. and his beautiful wife Talitha, in the laid-back atmosphere of Marrakesh.

Although Saint Laurent disliked international travel, he had long harboured a desire to return to the sunny climes and exotic colours of his North African childhood, which held vivid memories of happy times with his family. A holiday with Pierre Bergé, staying at La Mamounia in the hippy enclave of Marrakesh in 1967, had resulted in them purchasing a modest house located within the walls of the medina in a spot known as the Lemon Garden. The house was called Dar el-Hanch, which translated as "House of the Serpent", and was built around a stone courtyard several minutes away from the central square of Djemaa el-Fna.

OPPOSITE: Classic pin-stripe trouser suit, worn with an extravagant fox fur collar, photographed for a *Vogue* editorial in 1971.

ABOVE: Socializing
with the cool crowd at
Le Palace nightclub in
Paris, 1977, Yves Saint
Laurent with Pierre
Bergé to his left and
Andy Warhol on the
far right.

Marrakesh provided an opportunity for escapism, away from
Saint Laurent's demanding role as creative figurehead of his own
couture house, and the couple retreated there for several weeks at
a time as often as they could.

Under dazzling skies in the permissive culture of North Africa,
Saint Laurent could wander freely through the bustling souk,
dressed casually in sandals and a cotton kaftan, without being
recognized – in stark contrast to the daily duties required of him
in Paris. A heady cocktail of narcotics was readily available to
enhance the chilled-out holiday vibe. Kif – the local marijuana
of Morocco – was smoked openly, but opiates like heroin and
a new wave of hallucinogens were also popular among the chic
bohemian visitors. As documented in Alice Rawsthorn's 1996
biography *Yves Saint Laurent*, within the close confines of his
intimate group of loyal friends who often stayed with the couple,
Fernando Sánchez (a classmate years earlier at the Chambre
Syndicale), Clara Saint and her boyfriend, Thadée Klossowski
(son of the painter Balthus) and Betty and François Catroux,

Saint Laurent started experimenting with everything this relaxed environment could offer. As he explained years later to Anthony Burgess, "Drugs are more than an escape. They can open new imaginative vistas for the artist".

There was a dramatic feeling of change in Paris at the start of a new decade. President Charles de Gaulle had resigned after 11 years in power, America was still embroiled in the Vietnam War and the heady optimism of the sixties had been replaced with a darker cynicism. When Andy Warhol and his entourage of Factory disciples arrived in the capital in 1970, Saint Laurent had already acknowledged the American artist's cultural influence by referencing his work in his Pop Art collection. Warhol's crew were in Paris to shoot a short movie called *L'Amour* (1972) in Karl Lagerfeld's Left Bank apartment, with the German designer playing a minor role, and Saint Laurent visiting the set as a voyeur to mingle with the bohemian crowd of beautiful misfits. Warhol's underground art films were generally perceived as conceptual vanities, having low production values, dubious camerawork and baffling storylines, but always featuring a fascinating gang of creative people.

Saint Laurent and Lagerfeld had been youthful acquaintances since 1954 when the German designer came second in the International Wool Secretariat competition that had helped catapult Yves into his position at Christian Dior. Fiercely competitive individuals, as the success of YSL escalated, their friendship had somewhat soured and the polar differences in their respective personality traits had magnified to a point that they now existed in very different fashion cliques, with few people allowed to flit between both factions. Warhol knew both men but was captivated by the glowing magnetism that surrounded Saint Laurent, and in 1972 suggested he sit for a series of multicoloured silk screen portraits that captured the designer in reflective mood.

Paloma Picasso, who was living in Paris with her mother, the artist Françoise Gilot, was one of very few people who was allowed to hang out with the distinctly separate Saint Laurent and Lagerfeld fashion cliques. As a 22-year-old beauty, she presented herself in a way that was strikingly unforgettable: raven-black hair, porcelain skin and vivid red lips, all dressed up in an eclectic way that stylishly combined flea market finds from Portobello Road with pieces raided from her mother's wardrobe. Paloma looked remarkable in vintage clothes from the 1940s and often turned up wearing crepe de Chine dresses and elegant turbans which evoked memories for Saint Laurent of Christian Bérard's illustrations he had admired as a child, and also of the way his adorable mother

OPPOSITE: Inspired to produce his "Liberation" collection by the eclectic style choices of Paloma Picasso, who referenced the seventies decade with her Carmen Miranda turbans and silk tea dresses. Close friends of the designer, Paloma Picasso, Marisa Berenson and Loulou de la Falaise were placed strategically in the audience at the show to encourage support.

ABOVE: Photographic images taken by Helmut Newton from the 1971 "Liberation" collection, as well as the original 80 items of clothing were displayed at the Fondation Pierre Bergé – Yves Saint Laurent in Paris, in 2015.

OPPOSITE: Naomi Campbell in the Spring/Summer 2002 haute couture show, wearing a reproduction of the acid green fox fur "chubby" first seen as part of the "Liberation" collection that caused uproar.

Lucienne had dressed, back in Oran. It was these references that the designer was thinking of when he presented what came to be known as his "Scandal Collection" at the rue Spontini in January 1971.

The bombshell "Liberation" show inspired by 1940s wartime fashion quickly became known as "Paris's ugliest collection". It caused an uproar of disapproval from his regular clientele and an unprecedented wave of vitriol from the fashion press, who were shocked at the audacity of the 80-piece couture collection. Heavily influenced by retro fashion, first exemplified by the square-cut shoulders and boxy silhouettes adopted during the Second World War, Saint Laurent presented his audience with short dresses, wedge-heeled shoes, wide pleated pants and suits with square shoulders.

Support from friends Loulou de la Falaise, Marisa Berenson and Paloma Picasso, strategically positioned among the audience and wearing their own interpretations of this updated retro look, did little to counter the explosive reaction the show provoked.

Eugenia Sheppard, writing for the *International Herald Tribune*, did not hold back, proclaiming the collection "completely hideous", and even the French press attacked Saint Laurent for what they perceived as an unmitigated disaster in a way he could not previously have imagined.

Having championed an aesthetic style of elegant androgyny so successfully over recent years, the overt femininity of this collection, which featured sexy chiffon dresses with plunging necklines, short fox fur chubbies in garish colours, a velvet coat embroidered with red lips and puff-sleeved crepe de Chine dresses printed with erotic scenes from classical Greek art, provided a shocking departure from the traditional expectations of a Saint Laurent haute couture show. The models themselves appeared sexually blatant, visibly bra-less, heavily made up with red lips and nails and wearing chunky platform wedges, visual references that clearly stirred memories of the "horizontal collaborators" who slept with the Nazis under the Occupation. An overriding swell of anger was directed at Saint Laurent for reminding the middle-aged audience of their years lived in fear and deprivation, and the controversial show was described as "kitsch", the first time this word had been used in relation to bad taste vulgarity in fashion. The designer was prepared for the criticism and said in an interview with French *Elle* at the time: "I don't care if my pleated or draped dresses evoke the 1940s for cultivated fashion people. What's important is that young girls who have never known this fashion want to wear them."

In fact, the backlash was short-lived. Saint Laurent had broken the rules, drawing on nostalgia for a past he did not experience and representing it in a way that was bold, sexy and perfect for an audience of youthful women who demanded the right to choose their own style. The collection anticipated a new way of dressing that embraced ideas from a younger generation who casually mixed styles and influences from different eras, cultures and continents.

OPPOSITE: The fashion critics who sat in silence at the show declared the 1940s-style, silk slip dresses and crepe de Chine suits "hideous".

Drawing parallels with the negative response the artist Edouard Manet received for his painting *Olympia* when it was first exhibited in 1865, Saint Laurent understood that exploring new directions of creativity would inevitably attract criticism, as he explained to *Women's Wear Daily* after universal condemnation of his show: "I did not think that in a profession as free as fashion that one could meet so many people so narrow minded and reactionary, petty people paralyzed by taboos. But I am also very stimulated by this scandal because I know that which shocks is new."

In the wake of the Scandal collection, Nicaraguan-born Bianca Pérez-Mora Macías went to meet the designer for the first time in his offices in rue Spontini to commission her wedding dress, with a very clear idea of what she wanted. Unerringly modern, effortlessly chic and confidently assured of her own style, Bianca married Rolling Stone Mick Jagger wearing what was to become the most iconic wedding outfit ever seen. Paparazzi images of her sharp-shouldered, white tuxedo suit, worn with nothing but a glimpse of bare breast and an oversized sun hat, ricocheted around the world after the couple's quick ceremony on 12 May 1971 in the Town Hall in St Tropez.

Recalling the event nearly 40 years later, Bianca Jagger said, "Contrary to popular wisdom, it wasn't a trouser suit: it was a long, narrow skirt and a jacket. He made the wide-brimmed hat with a veil and we decided that instead of carrying a bouquet I should wear a flower corsage on my wrist to go with the suit." The 27-year-old groom – not known for his sartorial choices – was also wearing YSL couture, appearing alongside his partner in a pale green three-piece suit, dressed down with coloured sneakers. While marriage to Mick was brief and unsuccessful, Bianca remained a consistently loyal supporter and friend of Saint Laurent.

RIGHT: Extreme
tailoring exemplified
by the cut of the
exaggerated lapels in
this double-breasted
jacket worn with wide
legged pants, and a
decorative turban.

PREVIOUS PAGE:
Bianca Pérez-Mora
Macías marries Rolling
Stones frontman Mick
Jagger in St. Tropez
1971, in a white Yves
Saint Laurent tailored
two-piece suit and
broad-brimmed
white sun hat.

LEFT: Classic Yves Saint
Laurent blazer worn
over white 1940s-style
slacks, 1971.

RIGHT: Original Saint
Laurent sketches on
show at the Fondation
Pierre Berge – Yves
Saint Laurent, "Scandal
Collection" exhibition
in Paris, 2015.

Creating a scandal to generate publicity was a profitable idea. Later that year, the designer caused another storm by starring in his own advertising campaign for the launch of *Pour Homme*, the first YSL male fragrance. French fashion photographer Jeanloup Sieff, who was responsible for the monotone Christ-like image of an unashamedly naked Saint Laurent bathed in a halo of heavenly light, remembers the concept was fully formed when his friend arrived at the studio: "He told me to photograph him in the nude, he said he wanted to create a scandal. It was all Yves's idea."

Sitting cross-legged on a pile of black leather cushions and naked save for his trademark glasses, Sieff captured the serenity of a man confident of his own sexuality and produced an image that resonated with an audience of young gay men. First shown in the November 1971 issue of *Vogue Paris* and *Paris Match*, with other publications refusing to run the campaign, the resulting frenzy of press detailing the shockingly distasteful content helped fuel the flames of publicity, ensuring more sales and coverage than any amount of paid for advertising might have generated.

A new muse who clearly charmed Saint Laurent with her aristocratic heritage and wild bohemian style had recently been adopted into the inner sanctum, where she would remain as long-time confidante, creative "collaborateur" and partner in crime. Loulou de la Falaise was a part-English, part-French *enfant terrible*; a wafer-thin occasional model and fashion journalist who burst through the doors of Avenue Marceau dressed like an exotic nomad, laden with junk jewellery and trailing a multitude of scarves. She enchanted Paris and amused Saint Laurent with her madcap hippy deluxe London style and boundless energy, and as she worked alongside him for the next 30 years the designer relied on both her professional opinion and

OPPOSITE: Yves Saint Laurent with his long-time collaborator Loulou de la Falaise in a fashion shoot for *Vogue* shot by Deborah Turbeville.

personal friendship. The pair would often escape after long hour spent at the studio (along with the glamorous Betty Catroux) to let loose in a nightclub until the early hours of the morning.

Both women adored Saint Laurent and as Pierre Bergé confirms in the 2011 documentary *L'Amour Fou*, the feelings were mutual: "Yves was very fond of both of them, they played a very important part in his life." At work, Loulou would unfailingly bolster his spirits and spur him on by praising his latest ideas when black moods consumed him, while the relationship with Betty was darker, as she explained: "We had a very negative relationship. He'd call to say, 'Life is Hell' and I'd say, 'You're right!' I certainly didn't have a positive influence". The trio were often found dancing together till dawn at Le Sept, with the more sensible Bergé and François Catroux trying their best to act as strict parents to their younger partners, who behaved like uncontrollable teenagers. Their efforts invariably failed and as the decade continued, Saint Laurent's conduct became increasingly decadent and out of control, with the mental strain of having to produce four collections a year resulting in hysterical outbursts in the studio and progressively dangerous behaviour after dark.

As the physical dependency on drink and drugs became harder to disguise, the gossip columns regularly blasted out stories of breakdowns, incurable illness and even rumours of suicide and death. Everyone understood that Bergé would be around to pick up the pieces, handle the practical details of the business, shield his lover's lifestyle choices from public scrutiny, and present a public face of calm. But after one too many visits to the American Hospital to be treated for depression, drug and alcohol dependency, an obsessive affair with Lagerfeld's protégé Jacques de Bascher and a blazing row, where Saint Laurent

disappeared completely for 24 hours, Pierre called time on their relationship. Defeated by an 18-year professional and personal partnership that required constant management of Saint Laurent's fragility, he finally moved out of their rue de Babylone apartment in 1976, admitting, "It was very hard for me to leave Yves."

Left alone for the first time, an increasingly reclusive Saint Laurent was devasted by what he saw as abandonment and betrayal. In reality, the two men remained inextricably bound, both in a loving and loyal friendship and in their business dealings, with Bergé continuing to control the phenomenal success of the global empire they had built up together, while still protecting its most valuable asset.

THEATRE, BALLET
AND CINEMA

THE IRRESISTIBLE
ALLURE OF
THE STAGE

"If I wasn't a couturier I would have probably devoted myself to the theatre. The theatre's spell has appeared as a livelier, more radiant refuge than reality."

YVES SAINT LAURENT, 1959
(MUSÉE YVES SAINT LAURENT PARIS)

Throughout his life, Yves Saint Laurent complained bitterly that the fashion noose that weighed so heavily around his shoulders was a constant torment, even going so far as to tell a British journalist in 1977: "I hate fashion, I don't have any fun doing it. A show terrifies me."

If fate hadn't propelled a teenage Saint Laurent directly into the gilded environment of Christian Dior's salon, he may well have followed an alternative childhood dream and achieved comparable success in the magical world of entertainment – an early family trip to the theatre in 1950 had unleashed a passion that would stay with him for the rest of his life. Following this formative

OPPOSITE: Yves Saint Laurent with his friend, the choreographer Roland Petit, discussing costumes for Zizi Jeanmaire's Paris show *La Revue*.

experience of theatrical illusion, the teenager would spend hours alone at home, making cardboard characters wearing costumes he had designed himself, to perform in his "Illustre Petit Théâtre", a delightful miniature theatre he had constructed to put on plays for his sisters, Michèle and Brigitte. An adolescent Yves also spent time absorbed in literature, immersing himself in the poetic nostalgia of Marcel Proust, a discovery that would influence many future decisions. At the height of his fame it is thought Saint Laurent would book into hotels using the pseudonym Monsieur Swann (the protagonist of Proust's *À La Recherche du Temps Perdu/ In Search of Lost Time*) so as not to be recognized, and in 1983, he and Pierre Bergé purchased Château Gabriel, a lavish retreat in Normandy, where Bergé would deliver weekend guests by helicopter. Every guest room was identified with a brass door plaque naming a Proustian character.

The archives at the Musée Yves Saint Laurent Paris include many accomplished illustrations for costumes and stage sets that Saint Laurent produced at home in the early fifties for imaginary productions such as Jean Cocteau's *L'Aigle à Deux Têtes (The Eagle with Two Heads),* but his first professional commission came in 1956 when he was working as an assistant at Dior. Saint Laurent was approached to design the sets and costumes for *Le Bal des Têtes,* a flamboyant dressing-up ball that required attendees to wear an extravagant showstopper headdress. Hosted by the prominent aristocrat Baron Alexis de Rede, with a guest list that included every high society *grande dame* in Paris, this early invitation into the beau monde introduced the young couturier to many influential people, such as Hélène de Rothschild, Comtesse Jacqueline de Ribes and the Duchess of Windsor, as well as the acclaimed choreographer Roland Petit and his wife, the dancer Renée "Zizi" Jeanmaire. The couple became lifelong friends of the designer and they would go on to have many successful professional collaborations. The first came in 1959 with the ballet *Cyrano de Bergerac* at the Théâtre de l'Alhambra, with Saint Laurent designing all the sets and costumes and dressing the female lead, Roxanne, in layers of flouncy taffeta.

Though working nonstop in a demanding industry that required constant cyclical invention, Saint Laurent was a great lover of art and opera and took on many other projects during his 40-year career, creating costumes and sets for the theatre, ballet and cinema and winning many awards along the way. He worked with directors Claude Régy, Jean-Louis Barrault, Luis Buñuel, François Truffaut and dressed French stars of stage and screen Arletty, Jeanne Moreau, Isabelle Adjani and Catherine Deneuve, who remained a lifelong friend. The fantasy element of performance allowed him to indulge his imaginative creativity in a way that was often impossible within the commercial constraints of fashion, although visually, there were occasional signs of convergence between the disciplines. Most notably for Petit's ballet *Notre-Dame de Paris*, performed at The Palais Garnier, Opéra national de Paris, in December 1965, where the costumes for Phoebus were reminiscent of the Mondrian-inspired dresses he had first presented at his haute couture show earlier that year.

With the lithe body of a ballerina and lamp-post legs that went on forever, Zizi Jeanmaire was the perfect foil to pull off Saint Laurent's more outlandish showgirl costumes. Fusing burlesque tropes of feathers and sequins with a stylish aesthetic of elegance, the costumes he created for *Le Champagne Rosé*, a frothy pink confection of twinkling ostrich feathers, worn in her music hall show *Spectacle Zizi Jeanmaire* in 1963, perfectly exemplified the spirit of Parisian glamour. For *La Revue* at the Casino de Paris in 1970 the costumes became even more luxurious, with swathes of lavish fur, exotic palm tree plumes and topless dancers wearing thigh-high sparkly boots.

In 1965, Saint Laurent was introduced to Margot Fonteyn and Rudolf Nureyev, both of whom would become good friends, with the designer creating outfits for Fonteyn in both a professional and personal capacity. At her final benefit gala in 1990 the ballerina chose to bow out wearing a colourful YSL beaded couture dress.

Saint Laurent created costumes for many leading ladies of the cinema, starting with the wardrobe of Italian movie star Claudia Cardinale in *The Pink Panther*, a 1963 Hollywood comedy directed by Blake Edwards, but his most acclaimed cinematic collaboration came in 1967 with the wardrobe of Catherine Deneuve in *Belle de Jour*. Directed by the Spanish surrealist Luis Buñuel, 23-year-old Deneuve plays the bored housewife

OPPOSITE: Costumes for the principal dancers Roland Petit and Claire Mott in the 1965 ballet *Notre-Dame de Paris*.

protagonist Séverine Serizy, who enlivens her dull bourgeois lifestyle by spending her afternoons working in a high-class brothel. The neutral colour palette of modest costumes – the military vinyl trench coat with textural knitted sleeves, black shirt dress with demure white satin collar and cuffs and low patent pilgrim pumps with a silver buckle (produced by the shoemaker Roger Vivier) – became an integral part of the film's success and went on to become some of Saint Laurent's most iconic fashion staples.

Belle de Jour kick-started a long-standing friendship and the designer created costumes for Deneuve in François Truffaut's *La Sirène du Mississippi* (*Mississippi Mermaid*) in 1969, Jean-Pierre Melville's *Un Flic* (*A Cop*) in 1972 and Tony Scott's erotic vampire movie *The Hunger* starring David Bowie and Susan Sarandon in 1983.

In the mid-seventies at the height of fashion's obsession with the retro glam of 1920s and 30s Hollywood, Saint Laurent dressed Anny Duperey in a series of figure-hugging satin evening gowns and extravagant fox-fur shawls for her part as Arlette in Alain Resnais' biographical drama *Stavisky*. Having to create for both historical and futuristic projects on stage or through the medium of film gave him the freedom to invent a parallel universe that usefully counterbalanced the different demands of his considerable artistic output, something he readily acknowledged.

When in 1977 Pierre Bergé acquired and renovated the Théâtre de l'Athénée, and the following year staged the Cocteau play, *L'Aigle à Deux Têtes*, Saint Laurent was finally able to realize his childhood ambition, designing the sets and costumes for the romantic drama and receiving rave reviews for his resolute modernism and style.

OPPOSITE: Catherine Deneuve in her breakthrough role of Severine Serizy in Luis Buñuel's 1967 film *Belle de Jour*. Deneuve always acknowledged the importance of Saint Laurent's clothes in the film, describing the style as "timeless".

THE ICONIC PERFUMES

MODERN SCENTS

That a couture house could substantially boost both annual income and brand recognition with sales of a successful perfume had been well documented by the time Yves Saint Laurent diversified into this market.

*T*he early Parisian couturier Paul Poiret (1879–1944) had been subsidizing his bespoke fashion with the profits from a branded fragrance since 1910 and it was more than 40 years since Mademoiselle Chanel, for whom Saint Laurent had the utmost respect, had created the blueprint for Chanel No 5, the world's best-selling perfume. When US cosmetics giant Charles of The Ritz (who had bought out J. Mack Robinson's original investment in the Yves Saint Laurent fashion house) got in touch with Pierre Bergé with a proposal to oversee the production and marketing of a perfume bearing Yves Saint Laurent's name in return for a royalty fee of 5 per cent, the businessman was eager to strike a deal.

In spring 1964, Saint Laurent launched his first perfume using simply his initial "*Y*" (pronounced "ee-grec" in French) stencilled in gold on a square-cut modern bottle designed by Pierre Dinard.

OPPOSITE: The first perfume launched in 1964, simply named *Y*.

The light fragrance was created by Jean Amic of Roure perfumers using tuberose and ylang-ylang as mid notes and sandalwood, patchouli and oak moss as base notes. By the time an opportunity arose to expand the range, Charles of The Ritz had been sold to an American pharmaceutical group, Squibb-Beechnut, who agreed a deal to return the couture house to Saint Laurent and Bergé, while taking control of all new perfumes and agreeing a royalty payment. Saint Laurent wanted to create a fragrance targeted directly at the young women who were loyal fans of his ready-to-wear collections and in 1971, the company launched *Rive Gauche*, created by Jacques Polge, best known for his role as head perfumer at Les Parfums Chanel and considered to be one of the greatest "noses" of the twentieth century. With a name that was already recognizable as a result of the international success of the boutiques, marketing the product in an aluminium canister painted with silver, black and blue stripes (unlike any other perfume packaging of the time) and an advertising slogan that teased "Rive Gauche is not for self-effacing women", the fragrance resonated with a ready-made audience of independent women. Later that same year, the designer posed naked for the promotional campaign shot by his friend, the photographer Jeanloup Sieff, to launch his first menswear eau de toilette, *Pour Homme*. Though much in keeping with the zeitgeist of the time (the free loving hippies at Woodstock and the musical *Hair*) the figurehead of a luxury brand posing nude to sell his own products caused a terrific scandal and consequently huge publicity for the house and the fragrance. *Pour Homme* was a fresh and aromatic blend of bergamot and lemon verbena combined with base notes of amber and sandalwood to create a distinctly citrusy aroma.

Opium was promoted in Europe to coincide with the Opéras-Ballets Russes collection in 1977, but to celebrate the official

OPPOSITE: Marketed to reflect the design ethos of the ready-to-wear boutiques of the same name, *Rive Gauche* launched in 1971 and was presented in an ultra-modern striped tubular canister.

American photographer
Helmut Newton
captured Texan
model, Jerry Hall in a
seductive mood at Yves
Saint Laurent's Rue de
Babylone apartment
for the *Opium*
campaign in 1977.

ABOVE: A rare image
of Yves Saint Laurent
smiling, at the
extravagant launch
party for *Opium* held
on a Chinese junk
in Manhattan's East
Harbour.

arrival in America the following year, the Squibb Corporation threw a decadent party for Saint Laurent widely perceived as the "fashion event of the decade". The publicity stunt that cost an estimated $300,000 provided entertainment for 800 VIP guests on a spectacular Chinese junk called the *Peking*, moored in central Manhattan's East Harbour. Smiling like a superstar, the designer was surrounded all night by a handful of A-list friends (Diana Vreeland, Halston, Cher, Diane von Furstenberg) and a posse of perfectly groomed models, glittering in high-end couture. The fragrance, which had taken many years of research to produce, was an unusual blend of patchouli, myrrh and vanilla, presented in a unique bottle designed to look like an inro (a Japanese box with several compartments worn by the Samurai, fastened with a cord and closed with a netsuke, a small carved ornament of ivory or wood, to keep their spices, salt and herbal medicines).

The original Chinese "lacquer" packaging with gold lettering was suitably sophisticated, but the name *Opium* caused immediate outrage. Saint Laurent was accused of glamorizing drug use and the provocative advertising campaign shot by Helmut Newton and featuring American model Jerry Hall languishing seductively on a bed of cushions beneath the strapline, "*Opium*, for those who are addicted to Yves Saint Laurent" did little to detract from the charge. Having invested so heavily in the marketing campaign, Squibb were reluctant to respond to the criticism and rode out the protests, explaining that the name was evocative of the romance and mystery of the East. The ensuing press coverage boosted sales and *Opium* became an instant hit, with the initial stock selling out on both sides of the Atlantic.

Rudolf Nureyev, a close friend of Saint Laurent, seemed the
perfect choice to dance for an invited audience of 1,200 guests for
the launch of a new men's fragrance, *Kouros,* at the Opéra Comique
in 1981. The fragrance concept played heavily on themes of Adonis
as the word itself is the term given to the erotic nude sculptures
that first appeared in Ancient Greece. The press release for *Kouros*
read: "He is handsome like a God. He is handsome like a man. He
is the Absolute, the eternal beauty, the miracle, the revelation of the
Divine, true and simple grandeur". Renowned for his monstrous

ego and divine body, Nureyev danced flawlessly and when the performance was over, Saint Laurent surprised the audience by thanking his friend with a passionate mouth-to-mouth kiss.

Next came *Paris*, launched at the couture fashion show at the Hotel Intercontinental in 1983. At the runway finale, Mounia Orosemane, one of Saint Laurent's favourite models, strutted down the catwalk in a short shift wedding dress covered in birds-of-paradise plumes, clutching an oversized bottle of the new fragrance to present to the audience. *Paris* represented Saint Laurent's love letter to his city; the floral fragrance was tinged with the nostalgia of garden roses and the advertising campaign utilized the most iconic of Parisian landmarks, the Eiffel Tower, as a backdrop. As with previous perfumes, the name was controversial and the Paris City Council objected, ensuring publicity that only helped to boost sales, with *Paris* quickly joining *Opium* to become one of the top 10 bestsellers.

Jazz, an eau de toilette for men, was launched in 1988 with a stylish monotone advertising campaign featuring the cut-out silhouettes of jazz musicians harking back to Paris in the 1920s, one of the most decadent periods of French history. Saint Laurent's next perfume sold itself with the strapline "A Tribute to the Women Who Sparkle" and was packaged in a bottle designed to resemble a classic champagne cork. Launched in 1993 and called simply *Champagne*, the full-bodied perfume created by Sophia Grojsman (also responsible for *Paris*) was subject to legal scrutiny before it had even arrived in-store. Faced with a lawsuit from the Comité Interprofessionel du vin de Champagne (CIVC) for contravening the use of the word "champagne", which can only be used for a specific type of sparkling wine grown in one region, Saint Laurent was forced to rethink. *Champagne* was re-named as *Yves Saint Laurent* and then later in 1996, the perfume name was changed again to *Yvresse*.

ACCESSORIES AND JEWELLERY

ADORNED AND BEJEWELLED

"I like a dress to be simple and an accessory to be crazy."

YVES SAINT LAURENT
(MUSÉE YVES SAINT LAURENT PARIS)

Saint Laurent was a perfectionist. His early career with Christian Dior had instilled in him an understanding of the importance of a finished look – a signature hat, the right shoes, a discreet necklace – all of these accessories conveyed the formality of 1950s society expressed through haute couture fashion.

As an instigator of radical change, he was responsible for sweeping away the conventional codes of couture while still believing the overall expression of modernity he was creating required the requisite details of jewellery, scarves, gloves and hats to complete his vision and pull the whole look together. At show time he could be found backstage changing last-minute details, finding different earrings for a model to wear

OPPOSITE: Yves Saint Laurent trying out different jewellery on a model in preparation for the Christian Dior Autumn/Winter haute couture show in 1959.

ABOVE: Bespoke body jewellery created by the artist Claude Lalanne, for Yves Saint Laurent's Autumn/Winter 1969 collection.

with their outfit or swapping a handbag, demonstrating a passion for visual perfection that never waned. Early examples of his incredibly imaginative experiments with jewellery were produced in collaboration with friends, the artists François-Xavier and his wife, Claude Lalanne, to whom he had been introduced at the end of the 1950s through a mutual friend, Anne-Marie Muñoz.

On a visit to their studio, Saint Laurent had seen sculptural casts of torsos and chests which Claude Lalanne had made using a method called galvanoplasty. His imagination was fired, and for the Autumn/Winter haute couture collection of 1969, the sculptor made gold-plated metal castings from the body of the statuesque model Veruschka, which Saint Laurent incorporated into two stunning evening dresses made from diaphanous chiffon. Taking inspiration from the natural world, Lalanne continued to create statement jewellery for her friend until the early eighties, most notably the gilt bronze torque of the designer's own lips in 1970, intricate wisteria belts that wrapped decoratively around simple fluid gowns in 1971 and a spectacular range of headdresses in 1981.

An eternal theme of "love" permeated Saint Laurent's work, evident in the unique greetings cards he produced annually for friends, collaborators and clients from 1970 onward. The leitmotif for the house was a famous crystal brooch in the shape of an asymmetrical heart made of smoke-grey diamante encrusted with rubies and pearls. The oversized jewel, 12 by 8 cm (5 x 3½ in), was created by costume jeweller Roger Scemama for the first collection Saint Laurent produced under his own name in 1962. Initially worn as a statement necklace with a demure short evening dress, the piece became a good-luck talisman and was retained from one collection to the next, with other versions of the heart endlessly reinvented from 1979 onward in a myriad of materials, from wood to rock crystal.

On the day of the catwalk show the original heart necklace was delivered in a shoebox to Saint Laurent, who would decide who would be lucky enough to wear it – a tradition that became a hotly anticipated ritual in every show. Like Chanel, who detested precious gemstones and created a

trend for costume jewellery, Saint Laurent declared early on his preference for "*bijoux de fantaisie*", explaining at his first interview after winning the International Wool Secretariat prize in 1954, "I want to make daring accessories, 'couture' jewels that are so much more spiritual than real ones."

In the early seventies Paloma Picasso – who was making jewellery from beads bought at flea markets – was encouraged by Saint Laurent to make pieces for him, but it was Loulou de la Falaise, who joined in 1972, who would become a real asset to the company, dreaming up magical ideas in unorthodox materials that the artisan ateliers would skilfully turn into reality. At the beginning of a collection, Saint Laurent would set the theme and de la Falaise would immediately start the process of sketching out her own ideas, often juxtaposing strange materials like straw, plastic, glass or pebbles into her designs and working with the design team in the studio. With such madly inventive pieces becoming an integral part of the YSL style, the importance of jewellery escalated to the point that by 1990, the couture accessories were sold separately from the clothes in their own boutique on the rue du Faubourg Saint-Honoré. Saint Laurent was generous in acknowledging Loulou's input into his business, saying in 1984, "She is the real star among us, she strikes gold time after time with wonderful pieces of jewellery." The company utilized a wide range of specialist ateliers employing craftsmen who were experts in their own field to produce all of Saint Laurent's creative pieces. Robert Goossens, who had worked directly for Chanel and Balenciaga, produced rock crystal and gilt bronze, while Roger Scemama worked with wood, Augustine Gripoix produced *verre nacré* pieces, a mixture of poured glass and mother of pearl that set like pearl, and François Lesage created exquisite embroidery pieces.

PREVIOUS PAGE:
Sculpted torso and
breast imprints taken
from the model
Veruschka's body
were made in
galvanized copper by
Claude Lalanne, for
Yves Saint Laurent's
vibrant chiffon gowns.

RIGHT: Veronica Webb
on the catwalk in the
early 1990s, swathed
in gold jewellery, an
amber cuff and an
elaborate headdress.

LEFT: The famous heart created in 1962 by Roger Scemama became a house talisman that appeared in every catwalk show.

OPPOSITE: The butterfly motif, seen here as part of a decorative headpiece, was a recurring theme of nature, utilized as decoration on belts, earrings and brooches.

LEFT: Statement accessories used to offset the mannish cut of the trouser suit, Spring/Summer 1990 collection.

The Saint Laurent aesthetic played provocatively with colour and texture. The designer loathed the idea of coordinated accessories and often deliberately used contrasting materials and clashing shades to create impact. Hats made in-house were always an integral addition to the overall image.

"ONE CAN NEVER OVERSTATE THE IMPORTANCE OF ACCESSORIES."

YVES SAINT LAURENT, 1977, FRENCH ELLE

The conical "Chinese"-inspired hats for the Imperial China Autumn/Winter 1977 haute couture collection stunned for their simplistic shape executed in lavish brocade and fur fabrics, the fedora tipped perfectly across one eye became synonymous with the silhouette of his masculine trouser suits and many examples of the turban, either sleek and chic or wildly decorative, became a House staple throughout his career. Saint Laurent was experimental in both shoe and bag design, using a wide range of materials, including snakeskin, vinyl, plastic, velvet and the very best-quality leather and suedes.

Initially, shoes were made at Saint Laurent's own in-house workshops and later produced under licence. Quality was paramount, but he was also insistent that the flow of an outfit should not be interfered with by ill-conceived footwear. As such, everything he produced from the golden Cossack boots for the Opéra-Ballets Russes collection to the flat leather mules worn with his first pair of sailor pants was superbly crafted but extremely elegant.

ABOVE: Backstage
Loulou de la Falaise
puts the finishing
touches to Laetitia
Casta's outfit in
Yves Saint Laurent's
final show, January
2002.

By 1977, with the success of the company growing
exponentially, Pierre Bergé set up lucrative deals around
the globe to license the YSL name to numerous accessory
manufacturers. Saint Laurent agreed to sign his name to over
35 products, including scarves, jewellery, furs, sunglasses,
bed linen, shoes, umbrellas and even cigarettes, all of which
boosted the YSL brand while allowing the designer himself
to concentrate on what he did best.

RIGHT: Decorative earrings made up from strings of fake pearls, as Yves Saint Laurent was known to favour costume jewellery.

GLOBAL
INSPIRATION

INSPIRATIONAL JOURNEYS AROUND THE WORLD

"If you don't have the power of imagination, you don't have anything."

YVES SAINT LAURENT, 1978, WOMEN'S WEAR DAILY

As a successful young designer, Saint Laurent's revelation in 1968 that black was his favourite colour in response to the Proust Questionnaire, a set of 35 questions made famous by Marcel Proust and frequently used in interviews, came as no great surprise, given that much of his ground-breaking androgynous style depended on a subdued palette.

His modernist clean-cut lines of Summer 1975 featured 35 black designs from a collection of 74 outfits.

But Saint Laurent was a provocateur who liked to shock and his next, totally unpredicted, move unleashed a storm of superlatives. With an explosion of stunning theatricality performed to a sweeping operatic soundtrack, he revealed a new aesthetic that rejected his signature pared-down masculinity in

OPPOSITE: A luxurious take on traditional costumes inspired by the Ballet Russes for the Autumn/Winter ready-to-wear collection in 1976.

favour of dazzling fantasy. His winter 1976 Opéras-Ballets Russes collection captivated his audience, who were delighted by a parade of luxurious Russian peasant dresses, Cossack coats trimmed with mink, extravagant "babushka" gypsy skirts, jewel-coloured velvet bodices and gold lamé boots. The flamboyant presentation staged for the first time on a raised catwalk at the Hotel Inter-Continental in Paris received universal praise, with *The New York Times* proclaiming it "a revolutionary collection that will change the course of fashion" and the 40-year-old designer himself later conceding, "Perhaps it wasn't the best collection, but it was certainly the most beautiful." Inspired by the vast shelves of travel and art books pored over in his studio, he was continually drawn to the romantic themes of art and beauty from a bygone era. He explained to *Le Monde* in 1983 that his fantasy interpretations of a place were best explored by reading illustrated books from the safety of his own sofa: "my best journeys are in my imagination."

Time spent at his newly acquired pretty pink mansion Dar Es Saada la Zahia, "The House of Happiness in Serenity", located near the gorgeous Jardin Majorelle in Marrakesh, exposed Saint Laurent to a daily atmosphere of vibrant colour and sensuality. The traditional Moroccan dress of harem pants, tunics and hooded *djellabas* (long, loose-fitting robes with decorative embroidery worn by the locals in the medina) proved influential in his work, although subsequent "imaginary journeys" to investigate folkloric codes of Spain, China, India and Japan were just as impactful.

Twice a year he would stay for several weeks in Morocco, producing hundreds of preliminary sketches that included details of accessories and jewellery as the starting point for each collection. Saint Laurent drew quickly with a Staedtler 2B Graphite pencil or felt tip pens, but the demands on him to produce four shows a year (Spring/Summer and Autumn/Winter for haute couture and prêt-à-porter) continued to take their toll on his physical and mental wellbeing. His output for the Opéras-Ballets Russes show was prolific and Loulou de la Falaise spoke of his "total frenzy" when he returned to Paris with "4,000 beautiful drawings".

Preparation for a show followed a well-rehearsed system established over many years, which began by narrowing down hundreds of original research sketches into a workable, cohesive collection. Individual outfits were assigned to the specific *chefs d'atelier*, who would use their unique technical skill sets of dressmaking or tailoring to produce a "toile". This first fabric interpretation of the design made in ecru cotton and worn by the mannequin cabine (the fit model) would provide a realistic idea of what the final silhouette would look like. From the bright daylight studio on the second floor at Avenue Marceau the couturier and his collaborative team, which for 30 years included Anne-Marie Muñoz and Loulou de la Falaise, would inspect the toile

from every angle using the mirrored wall at the end of the studio to gain a different perspective.

After three or four toile fittings, the garment was ready to be made up in the sumptuous collection of fabrics ordered specifically for that season, many of them commissioned from Abraham, a Swiss silk company that Saint Laurent worked closely with. Rolls of satin, silk and mousseline filled every corner of the studio, with trimmings and fabrics for accessories chosen from sample books bursting with magnificent swatches of colour and texture. Having worked alongside Christian Dior, who relied heavily on stiffened interfacing to create shape, Saint Laurent banned it from his workrooms, relying instead on complex cutting techniques to create an outfit that he demanded must feel light and unrestrictive to wear.

From his inaugural collection in 1962, the designer was meticulous about keeping a factual record of every garment produced, something he continued to do until his resignation in 2002. In a book the team called "the bible" every item was included, from initial sketches assembled into a collection board named according to date and season, details of the *chef d'atelier*, fabric swatches, costs of materials, sales ledgers with details of customers purchases to photos of the model wearing the outfit.

The Opéras-Ballets Russes collection heralded a dramatic transformation in the overall aesthetic Saint Laurent presented, with every subsequent show becoming more staggeringly beautiful than the last. The Jamaican-born model and singer-songwriter Grace Jones opened the romantic Carmen collection inspired by an imaginary vision of Spain for Spring/Summer 1977. Paying homage to the Spanish artist Diego Velázquez, Saint Laurent had designed much of this show confined to his sick bed being treated for depression and addiction problems in the American Hospital of Paris in Neuilly-sur-Seine, but still succeeded in producing 280

OPPOSITE: Colourful embroidery and fringed shawls created for the Carmen collection, Spring/Summer 1977.

OPPOSITE: Gold Indian-inspired brocade and lavish embellishment for this "Shakespeare" wedding dress, from the Autumn/Winter 1980 collection.

RIGHT: Opulent fabrics and superb use of colour, showcased in Yves Saint Laurent's Imperial China collection, Autumn/Winter 1977.

outfits for a presentation that thrilled the audience for two and a half hours. Sexy velvet corsets, tiered layers of taffeta, fringed shawls, black lace mantillas and lacquered fans subverted the traditional iconography of the Flamenco dancer's wardrobe into something sensuously modern and gloriously colourful. A day after the show, Saint Laurent returned to hospital in another attempt to deal with his demons.

Tapping into unchartered cultural influences across the globe sparked new avenues of creativity in 1978 with the splendour of Imperial China, a collection commercially timed to coincide with the launch of Saint Laurent's new fragrance, *Opium*. Influenced by elements of traditional clothing, the designer created a fantasy interpretation of reality; the collection included wide-cut sleeves, asymmetric fastenings with embroidered tassels, short mandarin collars and millinery in the style of Asian conical hats, all made up in a stunning assortment of opulent gold brocades, jewel-coloured silks and the most extravagant mink-trimmed accessories.

Saint Laurent returned to the majesty of India in 1982, juxtaposing brilliant silk taffeta evening skirts with ornate turbans and intricate embroidery, having first presented Indian-inspired brocade coat dresses in 1962. Evidence of a Japanese influence then appeared in 1984 in the guise of short kimono-style jackets cut in a T shape, his use of oversized decorative bows in contrasting colours positioned on the backs of dresses, a stylish interpretation of the Japanese obi belt, the wide sash used to fasten a traditional kimono.

Saint Laurent was one of the first couturiers to celebrate diversity on the runway, working with black models such as Fidelia as early as 1962. From the seventies onward, his favourite house models included Mounia Orosemane, who said Saint Laurent had made her proud of the colour of her skin, Pat Cleveland, Iman, Rebecca Ayoko, Katoucha Niane and Naomi Campbell, who later credited the designer with getting her first French *Vogue* cover.

OPPOSITE: Long evening dress with contrasting oversized pink satin bow, from the Autumn/Winter 1983 collection.

THE LEGACY
OF YVES

A NATIONAL ICON

"Fame bought him nothing but suffering and more suffering."

PIERRE BERGÉ, 2010 (L'AMOUR FOU)

From the early 1980s, Yves Saint Laurent began a long, drawn-out process of withdrawal from public scrutiny, living an increasingly isolated existence surrounded by spectacular art and antiques in one of his many elegant homes, with only his French bulldog, Moujik III, for company.

In 1980, he and Pierre Bergé bought and lovingly restored a large 1930s mansion in Marrakesh called Villa Oasis, owned originally by the French artist, Jacques Majorelle. The property and surrounding six acres of Jardin Majorelle, filled with exotic cacti and palm trees landscaped around private ponds, provided an oasis of calm for the troubled designer. In 1983, the couple also acquired Château Gabriel, a Normandy retreat near the coast in Deauville, which reportedly cost $5 million and took several years to renovate in a style inspired by Saint Laurent's favourite Proust novel, *À La Recherche du Temps Perdu*.

OPPOSITE: Villa Oasis bought in 1980 in Marrakesh, in the colourful setting of the Jardin Majorelle.

ABOVE: Yves Saint Laurent provided a spectacular opening ceremony at the 1998 FIFA World Cup finals at the Stade de France, Saint-Denis with a fashion show featuring 300 models.

OPPOSITE: A vibrant colour palette, opulent prints and luxurious fabrics typified much of Saint Laurent's later work.

At 47, Saint Laurent was universally acknowledged as the most influential couturier of the twentieth century and as such was the first living designer to be honoured with a retrospective of his work at the Metropolitan Museum of Art's Costume Institute in New York. Instigated and curated by Diana Vreeland, it featured 180 exhibits from over a 25-year period and opened with a glittering $500-a-plate dinner for 800 VIP guests. The American fashion expert told *The New York Times* that the exhibition provided "an opportunity to show the work of a living genius." The 1983 show at the Met attracted around a million visitors and was followed by large-scale retrospectives in Beijing, staged in Paris at the Musée des Arts de la Mode in 1986, before travelling to Moscow, St Petersburg, Sydney and finally, Tokyo in 1990.

The success of the museum shows kick-started a trajectory that changed Saint Laurent's oeuvre, latterly dominated by tribute collections which often looked more like extravagant costume exhibits than modern womenswear. He paid homage to his own

work by re-presenting updated themes on Mondrian, the trouser suit, Le Smoking, and Le Trench, as well as acknowledging the talent of other famous artists showing collections that celebrated Picasso, Matisse, Shakespeare, the surrealist poet Louis Aragon and the witty 1930s couturier, Elsa Schiaparelli.

In 1990, the designer creatively recognized all the figures he had admired in life, including Marilyn Monroe, Catherine Deneuve, Marcel Proust, Bernard Buffet and, of course, Christian Dior. These runway shows, though no less spectacular, were played out in front of a fidgety audience, who waited anxiously to see if an expressionless Saint Laurent was capable of making it onto the catwalk, with many fashion commentators feeling his once-visionary contributions to a contemporary wardrobe were now long behind him.

Apart from the obligatory end-of-show appearance a couple of times a year, sightings of Saint Laurent were rare, although he did turn up to receive the numerous accolades bestowed upon him. In 1985 he was made Chevalier de la Légion d'Honneur by President François Mitterrand, then in 1999 the Council of Fashion Designers of America (CFDA) honoured him with a Lifetime Achievement Award; he received Italy's prestigious Rosa d'Oro Prize for artists in 2001 and was recognized again by his own country in 2007 when President Nicolas Sarkozy awarded him the Grand Officier de la Légion d'Honneur.

By 1990 Saint Laurent was drinking heavily again and ill enough to try another stint in rehabilitation, recounting both his hospitalization and detoxification programme to *Le Figaro* the following year as an experience that "changed my character".

With his partner's ongoing deterioration, Pierre Bergé worked tirelessly on a strategy to build a long lasting legacy for the brand he had helped create, seizing every opportunity to elevate Saint Laurent's status from that of genius couturier to a French national icon.

OPPOSITE: Yves Saint Laurent with Laetitia Casta at the 18th annual CFDA America fashion awards in New York, 1999.

LEFT: A new museum
dedicated to the life
and work of Yves
Saint Laurent opened
in Marrakesh in
October 2017.

For the 30th anniversary of the House in 1992, Bergé organized a gala event at the Opéra Bastille in Paris, where 100 models showcased three decades worth of iconic designs for 3,000 guests. The opening ceremony of the FIFA World Cup final in 1998 at the Stade de France in Paris featured a 15-minute Saint Laurent extravaganza, with 300 models from five continents strutting elegantly around the pitch to Ravel's *Bolero*, before floating seamlessly into the instantly recognizable YSL logo for the finale. The TV spectacular was watched by an estimated 1.7 billion viewers and made fashion history. Such was Saint Laurent's stature within France that his image was stamped onto the last franc coins produced before the introduction of the Euro in 2000.

Throughout their professional relationship he and Bergé understood their own roles perfectly, and it was Bergé who took control of all financial dealings, with the company having various owners over the years. In 1989 the YSL Group was successfully floated on the stock market with demand for shares far exceeding the offer. A few years later, in 1993, to safeguard against rising debts Bergé negotiated a £400 million transaction with the state-owned French pharmaceutical company Elf Sanofi, leaving both men exceedingly wealthy in a deal that surrendered the YSL perfume division, while they kept control of Yves Saint Laurent Couture. Five years later, Elf Sanofi sold to the Gucci Group, headed up by Domenico De Sole and Tom Ford, with an agreement that they would oversee the ready-to-wear and perfume divisions, with Saint Laurent happily in charge of haute couture until his retirement.

An emotional Saint Laurent held a press conference on 7 January 2002 in the salon at Avenue Marceau to announce his intention to retire from the profession he had given his life to. He spoke proudly of his achievements of the last 40 years and passionately about his commitment to haute couture:

RIGHT: Model
Claudia Schiffer in
an updated version
of the famous Le
Smoking, variations
of which appeared in
every catwalk show.

ABOVE: Celebrating 30 years of a successful career, with Pierre Bergé, Catherine Deneuve and Zizi Jeanmaire at the Opera Bastille, Paris.

"I have always placed a respect for this profession above all else. While not exactly an art, it nonetheless requires an artist for it to exist." The designer also talked openly about his drink and drug problems, placing them firmly in the past: "I have been through sheer hell. I have known fear and the terrors of solitude. I have known those fairweather friends we call tranquilizers and drugs. But one day, I was able to come through all of that, dazzled yet sober."

A fortnight later came his grand finale at the Centre George Pompidou, a two-hour show featuring a roll call of international beauties, including Carla Bruni, Jerry Hall, Naomi Campbell and Claudia Schiffer, who showcased a parade of 350 classic YSL designs taken from the archives, alongside new pieces from his Spring/Summer 2002 collection. The show ended with many interpretations of his most iconic piece Le Smoking, as the designer appeared to a standing ovation, with Catherine Deneuve and Laetitia Casta singing softly "*Ma plus belle historie d'amour, c'est vous*"/*My greatest love story is you*. When the last orders from the show had been made and delivered (all stitched with a special commemorative label) the couture house closed its doors forever, with only new ready-to-wear clothes designed by a creative director appointed by the Gucci Group permitted to bear the Yves Saint Laurent name.

Five years on from his retirement, on 1 June 2008, Yves Saint Laurent died of a brain tumour at his home in rue de Babylone, aged 71, with his lifelong friends, Pierre Bergé and Betty Catroux, by his side. His funeral, held at the seventeenth-century Église

BELOW: The rue de Babylone apartment where Yves Saint Laurent and Pierre Bergé lived, with an extraordinary collection of priceless art and antiques that were put up for auction after his death.

ABOVE: The final applause on the catwalk at the farewell haute couture show in January 2002 at the Centre Pompidou, Paris, flanked by Catherine Deneuve and Laetitia Casta.

Saint-Roch on rue Saint-Honoré (known as the artists' church), was a grand affair attended by French President Nicolas Sarkozy and First Lady Carla Bruni-Sarkozy alongside a host of fashion elites and his mother Lucienne and sisters, Brigitte and Michéle. Bergé spoke movingly of his longstanding soulmate, with whom he had recently entered into a formal civil union, and the designer's ashes were later taken to be scattered in the beautiful Jardin Majorelle in Marrakesh, where a memorial plaque was erected that simply reads "Yves Saint Laurent – French couturier".

With Yves gone, Bergé continued his work to cement an unshakable legacy for the exceptional man he called "an anarchist", who "remained subversive throughout his career." The Fondation Pierre Bergé – Yves Saint Laurent, which preserved thousands of haute couture garments, accessories and sketches, was established in 2002 and opened to the public in 2004 in the Avenue Marceau couture house, with plans for it to be turned into a permanent museum, alongside an equally impressive newly-build museum in Marrakesh. Geographically and architecturally, these monuments represented the flip sides of Saint Laurent's professional and private persona, but both would be dedicated to the heritage of the couturier, providing permanent exhibitions as well as curated experiences for paying visitors, while also acknowledging the vital role that Bergé played in the designer's international success.

One year after Saint Laurent's death, in what was dubbed "the sale of the century", Bergé put the extraordinary private collection of furniture, paintings, objets d'art and sculpture that the couple had amassed over a 40-year period under the hammer to fund his ambitious plans for the posterity of Yves Saint Laurent. The record-breaking three-day sale, which listed over 800 items, raised more than €375 million. Highlights included works by Piet Mondrian, Pablo Picasso, Edvard Munch, Paul Cézanne, Edgar Degas, Henri Matisse and Marcel Duchamp. Without a hint of nostalgia, Bergé also sold off Château Gabriel, a decision that sealed the final chapter of their complex journey together, with proceeds from the sales of Saint Laurent's personal homes and possessions used to secure his oeuvre within fashion history.

Pierre Bergé died in September 2017, aged 86, a month before he could witness the conclusion of his long-standing mission to pay tribute to the life and work of his partner. In October 2017, two YSL museums opened in Paris and Marrakesh, celebrating and consolidating the outstanding contribution Yves Saint Laurent, the most influential designer of the twentieth century, had made to contemporary fashion.

INDEX

RESOURCES

Benaim, Laurence, *Yves Saint Laurent: A Biography*, Rizzoli International Publications Inc, 2019

Berge, Pierre, *Yves Saint Laurent, Fashion Memoir*, Thames and Hudson 1997

Drake, Alicia, *The Beautiful Fall: Fashion, Genius and Glorious Excess in 1970s Paris*, Bloomsbury, 2006

Duras, Marguerite (introduction) *Yves Saint Laurent, Images of Design 1958–1988*, Ebury Press, 1988

Fraser-Cavassoni, Natasha, *Vogue on Yves Saint Laurent*, Abrams Image, 2015

Mauries, Patrick, *Yves Saint Laurent: Accessories*, Phaidon Press Ltd, 2017

Muller, Florence, *Yves Saint Laurent: The Perfection of Style*, Skira Rizzoli Publications, 2016

Ormen, Catherine, *All About Yves*, Laurence King Publishing, 2017

Palomo- Lovinski, Noel, *The World's Most Influential Fashion Designers: Hidden Connections and Lasting Legacies of Fashion's Iconic Creators*, BES Publishing, 2010

Petkanas, Christopher, *Loulou and Yves*, St.Martins Press, 2018

Rawsthorn, Alice, *Yves Saint Laurent: A Biography*, Harper Collins, 1996

Samuel, Aurelie, *Yves Saint Lauren, Dreams of the Orient*, Thames and Hudson, 2018

Vreeland, Diana (ed) *Yves Saint Laurent, The Metropolitan Museum of Art New York*, Thames and Hudson, 1984

L'amour fou, Director Pierre Thoretton, 2010
Yves Saint Laurent: The Last Collections, Director Olivier Meyrou, 2019

anothermag.com
guardian.com
museeyslparis.com
nytimes.com
numero.com
telegraph.com
wwd.com

CREDITS